A Father's Passing

By

J.D. Hunnicutt

Based on a true story

Dedicated to:

Anyone who has ever lost a parent

Or lost their way

ISBN# 978-0-578-03126-2

Chapter 1

It was a phone call David had expected to receive for over a decade, yet it was still a surprise when it finally came. He had just returned from another day working as an entertainer at a local theme park and was sitting on a well-worn couch in his tiny, one-bedroom apartment in Orlando, Florida. The caller ID on his phone read: PARENTS. It was unusual for David to receive a call from his parents. His normal routine was to call them on his drive home from work at the end of his week, which wasn't until Saturday. Today was Tuesday, December 23rd. David answered. His mother's voice greeted him. Her voice was different from any other time David had heard it. It was low and shook between each sentence. She informed David that his father, who had been in poor health since David was in high school fifteen years ago, had suffered a massive heart attack that morning while having coffee at a local cafe. The outlook was not good. The doctors were trying everything possible but nothing could be determined until the following morning. David tried to comfort his mother but, with him sitting in Orlando and his mother sitting in a small town in Oklahoma, there was only so much he could do. David's mother promised to call him as soon as she knew any more. David told his mother he loved her then hung up the phone.

His heart sank. His father had been doing so well, or so he was led to believe. This was so sudden. There was no time to prepare. Even though his father's state of health had always been at the back of his mind, David never expected this so soon; not at Christmas. He contemplated his mother's voice. There was a sense of finality in it that he had never before heard. This was not like the other times when his father had fallen ill. This was the first time David had not been by his mother's side. David sat in silence on his well-worn couch, alone, and thought.

David's thoughts drifted to all the times as a small child growing up in rural Florida that he accompanied his father to the local coffee shop there. Still having to leap up in order to sit on the counter stool, David sipped hot chocolate while his father, as was his routine, would tell the regulars of the small cafe that David was a little runaway that he found on the side of the road. David's father and his friends would smile and laugh as he continued his tale by saying that he was going to buy the poor boy a cup of hot chocolate before sending him back out and on his way. David would grin as he sipped and played along like a good son. David now thought about how he never told his father how frightening that story was to him. Even thinking about it now made David uncomfortable. He never knew why his father didn't at least once say that David was his son and he was proud to be seated with him. Now David was unsure if he ever would.

That night gave David little sleep. He knew that if the worst was to happen then he would have to drive to his parent's home in Oklahoma. Although David's parents had retired from Florida and moved to there over five years ago, David had never gone to visit them. One of his sisters and her husband lived in the same town; in fact they lived at the end of the same road. David had assisted his parents with everything when they lived near him in Florida so he had let time pass now that they moved. He had planned to visit but always found an excuse. David was good at excuses. He didn't have the money; he didn't have the time; he couldn't get away from work. David had found a way to make excuses for everything in his life. He reasoned his way out of continuing his education by becoming an actor working forty hours a week. He talked his way out of any serious relationship by making his life appear to be in a constant state of flux despite holding the same job in the same city for a decade. Now all David's excuses vanished. Now all David wondered was what would happen if his phone rang tomorrow.

<u>Chapter 2</u>

The next day David left his apartment and proceeded to go to work as normal. The Christmas holiday season was the busiest time of year for the theme parks. He never requested any of this time off. Too many of his coworkers with family and children wanted that time. David had no one and was not, in truth, a fan of Christmas. It was just a day when people spent money they didn't have on things they didn't need. It was something for little kids and parents who needed a day away from the drudgery of their jobs. David arrived at the parking lot and began the long walk across the park to where his work trailer was placed. Through the dark sunglasses he wore, David watched the families around him closer than he normally did. Usually the park guests that surrounded David were a faceless sea of humanity. He had been walking through the same crowd five days a week for ten years. This routine had left David with a sense of distain for these families. He saw the exact same thing every working hour of every day. Families arguing with one another while torrents of sweat ran down their sunburned flesh. Their faces all blurred together long ago. However today, on this Christmas Eve, David watched them closely from behind his anonymous glasses. Today, for the first time since before he could recall, he saw their happiness. He saw their joy. He saw fathers with their sons held high upon their shoulders. David thought of his own father, still unsure as to what fate had in store.

As soon as David arrived at his trailer, he walked into his manager's office, closing the door behind him. David's manager was a former performer and an old friend of his, which made the telling of his situation more bearable. Compassionately as any man could be, David's manager assured him that despite the holiday, all arrangements would be taken care of if in the fact David should receive the news he dreaded. David thanked his manager, composed himself, left the office and continued to begin his day as if it was just like any other.

Chapter 3

David's job was to act and dance in a children's live action character show in the theme park. The normal show was transformed every December into one that reflected the political correctness guidelines of the park, while still trying to convey the spirit of the season. It was a show that David despised doing. Part of David's holiday costume was a heavy faux fur Santa coat. David had to wear this while he danced and entertained, despite the fact that the temperature in December in Florida in the center of the vast asphalt park seldom dropped below 80 degrees. The only thoughts that gave David comfort during this time were that it was only for a month and at least he wasn't trapped in one of the furry animated character suits. It was little comfort at best.

David returned to the trailer after his first show. He quickly removed his costume and held his head under the water running into the bathroom sink in order to attempt to remove the sweat from his face and hair. The water would run into David's mouth, where he could taste the tint of salt from his perspiration. David toweled off his head and changed into a dry shirt and matching shorts, which were provided by the company as undergarments. These clothes not only were comfortable but also kept him from having to use his personal clothing. David opened his locker to retrieve his phone. He had missed one call and one voice mail message was left. Both were from his sister who lived at the end of his parent's road in the small town in Oklahoma. David calmly walked past his fellow coworkers and went outside to listen to the message.

His sister's voice was filled with tears. She told her brother that their father's situation was dire and that David should call her immediately. David deleted the message. He drew a deep breath into his quivering lungs before returning his sister's call. She answered on the second ring. David's sister told him that their father had not been able to be revived. He was brain-dead and was currently being kept alive solely by machines. David absorbed this news and replied with the only words he could force from his throat. "I'm on my way."

David' sister told him to hurry but be careful. David

didn't hear her. His phone fell away from his ear. David sat down on a cement block at his feet. His phone dropped from his weak grasp, landing gently onto the hard cement. David thoughts immediately went to the last time he saw his father. It was the day his parents moved to Oklahoma. The last thing he did was shake his father's hand. He hadn't hugged his father or told him that he loved him. He just shook his hand. David placed his head into his own hands and began to cry. He had not cried for anything in a very long time. In David's mind, for a man to cry was a sign of weakness. Despite this; despite now being a man in his thirties, David now wept as if he was once again a little boy.

Chapter 4

After a few minutes, David controlled his breath and stopped his tears. He picked up his phone and dashed back inside his work trailer. He made eye contact with no one, but proceeded directly into the rest room. Once again David washed his head under the sink's flowing water, only this time the tinge of salt came not from the sweat of his brow but from the sadness overflowing his heart. He dried his eyes, removed his work garments and dressed again in his personal clothes. By this time, David's manager had entered the rest room. David told him what his sister's message had said. David's manager told him that all the arrangements for his absence were taken care of and not to worry. David told his manager that he would return to work on the following Tuesday, which was when his next scheduled week began. They shook each other's hands, and then embraced. David placed his dark sunglasses over his eyes and exited the trailer past his on looking and confused coworkers.

David returned to his apartment and turned on his computer. He typed his parent's address into a search engine and printed the directions to a place he had never been. The printed pages informed David that the trip was over 1200 miles and would take over 19 straight hours to complete. David looked at the time. It was already 1:07 PM on Christmas Eve. Moving swiftly, David packed some clothes and essential toiletries into a carry-on size piece of luggage he removed from his closet. He filled a plastic grocery bag with two bottles of water and some bread to sustain him until he arrived at his distant destination. As he was doing this, he felt something warm, furry and familiar rub against his ankles. His cat, Moses, purred. He was happy to see his master home early. The pain in David's mind had made him forget about the little stray he had rescued nearly two years ago. He had no time to make arrangements for Moses's care over the days David had to be away. With no other option, David threw a bag of cat food into his plastic bag. David picked up Moses's litter box along with the one piece of luggage and carried them out of his apartment. He arranged the items in the cab of the tan Ford Ranger he drove, leaving the passenger seat open for Moses. David returned to his apartment and picked up his beloved cat. "At least", David thought, "I'll have you for company." David walked out, locked the door of his apartment and opened his truck again. He climbed inside and softly petted the confused Moses in an attempt to comfort him. David read over his printed directions one more time then started his truck. He sighed at the thought of what lay ahead of him, and then drove away from his apartment under the bright Christmas Eve sun.

Chapter 5

The sun began to set in the western sky. David had
pulled into a small gas station off of the interstate somewhere in
Georgia. As he was waiting for his truck to finish refueling, he
gazed toward the violet horizon. He wondered if the sun had
begun to set in Oklahoma. He thought of his mother watching
the same sun. The nozzle of the gas pump stopped. David
placed it back then walked into the store. Although he had
never been a fan of energy drinks, he decided to buy a few. The
bread had brought had already been eaten and anything that
would help him fight off sleep this night was appreciated. He
purchased the drinks plus a candy bar then headed back to his
truck. His truck was over ten years old and although David did
everything he could to keep it in the best shape possible, he
wondered about its ability to survive this trip. David had never
driven his truck this far. At this point, however, those thoughts
had to be kept away. David knew he would need every bit of

his focus to get him through this night. He opened the door to his truck. Moses, who had decided to stay under David's seat, scurried away from the opening door. David smiled. At least he wouldn't have to worry about his frightened companion escaping. He placed the items he had purchased on the empty seat he had assumed Moses would use. David started his truck and turned back onto the interstate, eager again to put more miles behind him.

The onset of night provided David with an opportunity to think. Because it was Christmas Eve, very little traffic accompanied him on the road. The only other people he saw were interstate truckers. How much were they getting paid to travel on this night? Were their families waiting for them in some distant city? Did they have a family? David did. He had a brother and three sisters. All of them were raised in Florida but they had each long since scattered around the country. All except for David. Being the youngest, he had been left to stay in Florida, which was fine with him. Despite the rare e-mail or letter, David had not spoken with his siblings for many years. It wasn't that he didn't feel a sense of love for them. Long ago David had let the weeks without contact turn into months; then the months turned into years. After such a lapse in time, David didn't even know how to begin the conversation if he had wanted. When they were young, they had all been bound by a strong Christian upbringing. His brother and sisters had stayed strong in their faith but, as he grew older, David hadn't found much use for the church in his life. Between the late nights out with friends and the joy he found in the secular pleasures of the world, church quickly became an uncomfortable and seemingly judgmental place for him. As he became an adult living on his own, Sundays had easily been transformed into a day of sleeping in and watching sports. This had created even more distance with his family. David detested when he was asked why he no longer attended church. He was an adult now and made his own decisions. Religion never even entered his mind any more. He couldn't even recall where he last placed his Bible. He was sure it was still somewhere in his apartment. It was probably under a pile or buried in a box somewhere in his closet. David hadn't thought of his Bible in years.

Chapter 6

It was approaching midnight. David was now driving through Mississippi. He had never been here before but, living in the South, he was familiar with the stories and jokes that always accompanied this state. Alone driving down the highway, David noticed that Mississippi was much prettier than he had ever imagined. The dark hills that surrounded him were covered with groves of trees. How beautiful they must be during the day! At the mere thought of daylight, David remembered how long it would be until he saw the sun again. A thick wave of fatigue rolled across his body. Although he hadn't seen a rest area since he entered this state, David had noticed a few trucks that pulled underneath the overpasses along the interstate in order to rest. David saw an empty overpass ahead. He pulled underneath and shut off his truck. A few minutes to recharge himself could be spared. David reclined across the empty seat next to him. Moses jumped up and stood on David's chest. David smiled at his friend. Moses stretched and reclined on David, who stroked his soft gray fur. David stared up at the sky above him. There were no lights for miles. He was amazed by how beautiful the stars were. Living in the city, he had forgotten how many there were and how brightly they shone in the sky. David glanced back at the clock. It was 12:03 AM.

It was now Christmas Day. At least technically it was. It was a day that hadn't meant anything to him in many years but this was different. David looked back up into the sky. The last time he had seen a night filled with this many stars was when he had been a young boy. Back then, every night shone like this. Back then Christmas had still been a time of magic and wonder. David thought back to how his father would read the Christmas story from the Bible. Then the family would head off to bed, where sleep was mixed with growing anticipation until dawn when everyone would race back downstairs. David's father would hand out the presents as his mother would start cooking breakfast. After the presents were opened and the breakfast was cooked, the family would gather around to eat. They all would bow their heads while David's father blessed the food and reminded the family to remember the birth of the Savior on this special day. As David stared up past the overpass and into the vast Mississippi night, he could taste that breakfast. David hadn't celebrated Christmas for many years. He always worked. Christmas had become just another day to him. The importance of Christmas had faded from David's life just like the bright stars he now stared at had. These bright stars had awoken long dormant memories in David. For the first time in years, David missed being with his family. He thought of his father lying in a far-distant hospital. He thought of his mother being alone in her house for the first time in nearly fifty years. David sat up. Moses immediately leapt back down to his chosen place under David's chair. He had to make it soon. Opening one of the energy drinks, David took a long draught then drove back out into the night.

Chapter 7

The city of Memphis greeted David a little over an hour later. The tall buildings that created its skyline were dark and empty. David had just finished refueling again. The station had only one attendant inside. She was an older lady. David guessed her to be in her middle to late fifties. Why was she here, working this early on Christmas morning? David wondered about her family. Didn't she have someone to care for? Someone to care for her? He hoped that she did. Maybe they were waiting for her to come home. David knew his own mother was waiting for him. As he made his way from one empty interstate onto another, David thought of his mother. He had been the only child still living at home the first time his father fell ill. He had been a sophomore in high school at the time and knew that his father had been in failing health but being a teenage boy, David hadn't given his father's condition then much thought. His father was always so strong; David had believed him to be impervious to the weaknesses that befell other men. That is until that single, fateful day.

David had just walked into his home from another day of school. He was exhausted from football practice and the thought of homework still to do loomed over his mind. David found his mother standing alone in the living room. She turned to David and told him that his father had been taken to the hospital where he was now unconscious in the intensive care unit. David's mother threw herself into her son's arms and cried.

As he drove down the empty highways of Memphis, David remembered how his mother told him through her tears that she didn't know what she was going to do. All he wanted to do then was cry with her but, for the first time in his life, David knew he could not. He had to be the strong one at that moment. His mother needed him. David remembered that he prayed for strength then. As he crossed the bridge spanning the mighty Mississippi River on this dark Christmas morning, David thought about that prayer and the comfort and solace it gave him at that time. The strength it supplied to a teenage boy faced with his mother's tears and his father's mortality. David thought of when he last prayed. He couldn't remember.

Chapter 8

The hours past slowly for David as he drove through Arkansas. Moses was sound asleep. David envied his little companion. The drinks he purchased back in Georgia had long been emptied. David cursed the lack of energy that they truly brought. Weariness flowed into him with every breath. He turned up the radio in his truck, as if the volume alone could keep him alert. He hadn't realized that crossing into the Central Time Zone would delay the dawn an extra hour for him. This night seemed endless. David wished for his bed. He wished his father was well and that this trip would never had to have been undertook. The years since David had last seen his father seemed to be many more now than they actually were. David spoke on the phone to his parents once a week. Up until now, David thought that was enough. He had always planned to visit them one day. As he drove through this endless Arkansas night, David cursed himself for making the effort sooner.

His father had been doing so well. Every week David spoke to him, he had sounded stronger. David thought he had plenty of time to see his father again. Now he knew that those days had come to an end. It was an end David had never truly prepared himself for facing. He glanced back into the rearview mirror. Why wouldn't the sun rise? Little Rock was as dark and empty as Memphis had been. The road never changed. The only light David had seen for hours were from his own headlights and the lights of truckers passing him. At that moment, David would have given anything for Christmas morning to come. In every town David passed, he imagined the children living there waking up with joy in their hearts. He imagined their fathers handing out their presents. He remembered his own father, now brain-dead and being kept alive only through the assistance of machines. If only the dawn would come! David knew it would give him the strength to continue. He wished he could hold his mother at this very moment. He wanted to be able to give her the help she cried for him to give her those many years ago.

Suddenly a single, intense thought entered David's mind. A burning idea that David never had imagined would enter in again. David, desperate and alone with his heart in his throat, prayed. He prayed to God to give him the strength now he had given him as a young man. He prayed to give his mother comfort until he arrived. David prayed as if he never had before. "Please, God, please see me through this night! If only for my mother's sake. Please, God, please...help me." David hadn't noticed but a tear ran down his face. He wiped it away and refocused himself on the road ahead. David looked behind him once again. Over the rolling hills of the Arkansas countryside, thin rays of red and purple sunlight ran up the black sky from the horizon behind him. Dawn had come at last.

Chapter 9

The sky was now bright yellow as David drove through the Oklahoma countryside. He was, as near as he could figure, about an hour away from his mother's home. She and David's sister were already at the hospital in Oklahoma City, waiting for David to join them at their father's side. He had just gotten off the phone with his brother-in-law, who was staying in the small town in order to let David into his mother's home before driving them both to the hospital. The anticipation of arriving was now equaled by David's exhaustion. He had been driving for over twenty straight hours. The time he had lost through gassing up his truck and stopping for short breaks at the rest areas had added up. It would all be worth it though, once he arrived. The fact that it was Christmas had slipped away from David's mind. All he could think of was of no longer driving; of not staring at the road ahead.

At last, the exit David had sought for nearly a full day

appeared. David turned onto a thin ribbon of asphalt that extended south into the Oklahoma heartland. David picked up his phone and called his brother-in-law, who informed David he would be waiting at his mother's home. The minutes now dripped by even slower. He drove into the small town, which to David appeared nearly abandoned. He turned onto the appropriate street and immediately saw his brother-in-law standing in front of the modest blue and white, ranch-style house his parents called their own. David pulled in and stopped his truck. He breathed a heavy sigh of relief. He had made it. David had arrived.

Chapter 10

David's brother-in-law let him into the house. Although David had never been there, he recognized the lifetime of memorabilia that he knew a boy. His mother had the same piano, the same wooden cabinets and the same pictures hanging on the walls. His brother-in-law led him down a short hallway to the room which was prepared for him. David set Moses's litter box and his food and water dish in the adjoining bathroom. The poor cat was so relieved to be out of his travelling prison. He sniffed and investigated his new surroundings. The hospital in Oklahoma City was still a forty-five minute drive away but David desperately needed a proper bathroom, a shower and a change of clothes. David's brother-in-law said he would wait while David refreshed himself.

Closing the door to the room, David collapsed onto the bed. He took a moment and closed his eyes. He thought about the hours and miles behind him. He thought of his mother and his sister who were right at that very moment in the hospital with his father. David knew that the time for him to rest was not yet at hand. Drawing himself up, David opened his small suitcase, removed some clean clothes and went into the bathroom.

Moses greeted his tired master with a warm purr. David noticed that Moses had quickly made himself at home, having already eaten and used his litter box. The sight of his cat's now empty food dish made David realize that he himself had not eaten anything that could remotely be called a meal for almost a full day now. Ignoring his hunger, David turned on the shower and stepped into the warm stream of water. It was so refreshing. The miles he had traveled rolled away with each drop. Mentally, he used this brief respite to try and prepare himself to see his father. David had seen his father immobile in a hospital bed before but never in such a hopeless state. He would have to be strong, both for himself and his mother. David recalled the prayer he had made earlier that morning. Did it really work and had it been just coincidence? David hadn't seen much in his life over the last few years to convince him that religion and prayer did any good. For David, alcohol was a much quicker and surer way to ease his daily problems. David turned the water a bit hotter. He knew that here, alcohol was about as far away for him as his apartment in Florida. He was back into the Christian household in which he grew up. David knew his lifestyle over the next days would be tested. Not only with the stress of helping his mother with whatever she needed but also with the suppression of his own vices. That was something David knew he would be forced to face, but not now. Now he had to go to his father's side. David shut off the water and dried himself with one of the towels left out for him and changed into the fresh clothes. The water and brief time had rejuvenated David enough to face the trial ahead. He combed his hair and gave Moses a pat on the head before exiting the bedroom, shutting the door behind him.

David's brother-in-law was waiting for him in the living room. He had made David a ham and cheese sandwich for the ride to the hospital. David's stomach churned at the sight of the mouth-watering food. The two men left the house and climbed into David's brother-in-law's large Suburban. These seats were much more comfortable than the ones in David's small pickup. David wished this was the vehicle he could have driven here in but he was content to enjoy the comfort now. The sandwich, to David, was one of the greatest he had ever eaten. As he savored each bite, David's brother-in-law filled him in on the previous days' events. David's father had suffered a massive heart attack. The doctor said all four heart chambers had begun to contract independently of one another. By the time his father arrived at the hospital, the doctor informed the family that there was virtually no chance of resuscitation. The lack of oxygen had caused repeated strokes on top of the heart attack itself. Even if by a miracle he were to survive, David's father would have no way to function on his own. David could not imagine his father in such a state. His father had been the cornerstone of strength for his family. Even after his first incident and the subsequent hospital stays, David's father always bounced back with the same strength and humor. David had a hard time believing that this was the end.

David's brother-in-law went on to tell David, who was finishing the last of his precious sandwich, that some members of the church would be dropping in tomorrow to visit his mother. The thought of this made David's heart skip. What would he say to these people, who had known and loved his parents in his absence? David was here now; he was to be his mother's strength, just like he was in the years before. This was a thought for tomorrow, however. The hospital was now only minutes away. David had to prepare himself for what he knew he never could. He had to prepare himself to watch his father die.

Chapter 11

Hospitals had always been a problem for David. When he was only four years old, he shattered his left elbow. It took two surgeries and a pair of screws to put his arm back together. It was a memory that still haunted David occasionally in his dreams. Before, whenever he would accompany his mother when she visited his father in the hospital, David would inevitably become light-headed and nauseous by merely standing in the room. As David now walked toward the tall glass doors of this hospital's entrance, he thought of those incidents. He looked down at his left elbow and the physical scar that was now thirty years old but still visible. On this day there could be no fear. There could be no apprehension. This was a time for David to summon his strength and be the man his father raised him to be.

David stepped into the hospital. All hospitals smelled the same to him. It was an ill and irritating mixture of sickness and sterilization. David swallowed hard into his throat. He followed

his brother-in-law into an awaiting elevator. Unconsciously, as

the elevator doors closed the two men in, David found himself

asking God to see him through this. That made two prayers in

one day. He hadn't done that since he was a small boy. Still,

David found himself breathing easier than he ever before had in

a hospital. His brother-in-law placed an arm up onto David's

shoulder and asked him if he was ready. David said he was.

The time was at hand. The elevator doors opened. David

followed his brother-in-law out.

Chapter 12

The room of his father was only a few doors down the hallway from the elevator. David's sister stood by the entrance. Over the last ten years or so, this was the sibling with which David had the least contact. As a matter of fact, other than their conversation a day ago, they had not spoken since before David could recall. His sister embraced her husband. David walked past them both and into the room. He had thought of this moment since he had left his apartment so many miles ago. He could wait no longer.

The sight of his father, which up until now was left to imagination, met David's eyes. Tubes and wires ran from every part of his prone father into a variety of humming machines. His father's eyes were open but completely vacant in a way that David had never seen in a human being. The mouth of his father was frozen half-open. Every second or two, his father's head would twitch and shudder. With one look, David knew that whatever he had known about this man, whatever it was that made his father his father, was gone. There was a terrible absence in the form that laid before David's eyes. David had long ago given up the notion of a soul. It was a child's tale. Something parents told kids to comfort them, like Santa Claus or the Tooth Fairy. Upon gazing upon his father now, David knew he was wrong. There was something great and powerful missing. David's mother, who had been seated next to her husband, stood and embraced her son. To David, it felt just as it did the first time his mother asked for his help. Only this time, there were no tears in his mother's eyes. David's mother whispered softly into his ear. "He's gone." David answered back, "I know, Mom. I know."

Chapter 13

The four of them stood around their father's bedside. The conversation switched to David's journey. His mother was happy he had made it safely. She said she was surprised that he left so immediately to make it to his father's side, especially at this time of year. She told David that one more of his sisters would arrive on the evening tomorrow, which was welcome news to David as he had planned to depart the morning after that. David told his mother that he could not stay away from work any longer than that. This was the first moment that David took the time to think about his decision. He had never questioned coming; he had only came. He never thought until this moment of why. He had been the one separated from the rest of his family. His brother had not come. No one else had. Only David dropped his responsibilities and came. He looked over at his mother. In her eyes, David found his reason. He was the one who had been there the first time. He was the one who had to be here now.

A nurse entered the room and introduced herself to David. She informed the family that now was the time to decide their father's fate. Without hesitation, David, his sister, and most importantly his mother all agreed that their father was not in the shell of flesh that lied on the bed before them and it was time to end it. The nurse remarked that it was odd to see a family with such resolve. Most families, the nurse said, held onto the body no matter how hopeless the situation was, weeping and begging for more time. As David held his mother's hand, the nurse shut of the machines that kept his father's body alive one by one. She said that the time for the body to actually expire once the machines were turned off varied, but she did not expect a man in their father's condition to last very long. As the machines grew silent and stopped, the nurse left the room.

David's mother began recalling her favorite moments spent with her beloved husband of almost fifty years. Soon David and his sister were adding their own stories as well. The room, which David had assumed would be filled with deep loss and sadness, was instead a place of warmth and comfort. For over a half of an hour, the family spoke and told tales, all the while their father's vital signs continued to remain relatively constant. Every few minutes, the nurse would check in and be amazed not only of their father's body unwillingness to expire but also of the warm spirit of love in the room. When he was not retelling stories, David would glance over to his father's body. He had dreaded the feeling of loss that he expected to have for so long but it was not there. David felt only love. A love he had not found in any bottle or with any woman. It was a love so encompassing that David forgot all about the trials he undertook to get here.

Finally David's brother-in-law suggested that the other three go down and get something to eat. David's mother and sister had not eaten at all this day and the sandwich David inhaled was not nearly enough. The three agreed under the stipulation that David's sister would be called the instant anything changed with their father. David took his mother by her arm and the three exited the room.

Less than a minute later, as the three were waiting for the elevator to arrive, David sister's phone rang. The three raced back into the room immediately. All of their father's vital signs were at zero on every machine. The levels that had remained stable for so long were all flat-lined. David's brother-in-law, who was seated next to their father, told them that as soon as they left, the room suddenly felt colder. Then in an instant, all of the levels of the machines dropped to zero. He said that it was as if their father waited as long as they needed him and listened to their stories. When they left the room, David's father knew it was time to depart. David held his mother until she broke away and went to her husband's side. She picked up his hand then muttered, "He's so cold."

A doctor entered the room. He performed the necessary routine checks then officially pronounced David's father dead. The doctor left as quickly as he came. He was soon replaced by another doctor, whom was recognized and embraced by David's sister and mother. This doctor, David noticed, had tears welling up in his eyes. The doctor shook David's hand and introduced himself as his father's personal physician. "Your father", the doctor told David, "was my favorite patient. He always responded to his situation with a sense of humor and confidence that I have never seen before. I'm sorry I couldn't do more." David had never expected to find such a genuine feeling of grief and loss in the eyes of a man whose job it was to tend to the sick and who encountered the specter of death every day. David thanked the doctor for all he had done. The doctor asked David's mother if any arrangements had been made. David's mother smiled and said that members of her church had already arranged for the body to be transported to the selected funeral home. This was a task that David had assumed would fall upon him. He was relieved to hear it would not. The doctor hugged David's mother and sister again before exiting. The four family members took one last look upon their father then left the room. They all walked silently to the elevator and waited for it to arrive.

Chapter 14

Inside the elevator, David asked his mother what she wanted to do. She replied that it was all over now and she wanted to go down to the commissary. Being Christmas, the nurses had informed her that the meals today were free. The elevator opened and David and his family walked down the hall. They made their way over to the buffet that was set up. Each one took their tray in turn. The choices were few but all of them appeared tasty. David made sure his mother got her tray around to every item. He was amazed at his mother's poise at this trying time. After their trays were filled, David carried both his and his mother's over to where his sister and her husband already sat.

Being Christmas, very few other families were present. One in particular caught David's eye. In a hushed voice, David's mother told him that they were losing their grandfather today. The family David watched ate their food in a somber silence. Each of those family members looked distressed and intensely troubled. David then brought his attention back to the table where he sat with his family. They had each just experienced the same loss the other family feared but there was no sign in David's family of melancholy. They just discussed what they had to do for the remainder of the day. David's mother had transformed her thoughts of loss to ones of David's well-being. She wanted to return home so David could get some rest. David wondered if his appearance led his mother to her concern. They all decided to gather at their mother's home tomorrow morning. Finishing their meal, David and his family left the sanctuary of the hospital and climbed back into the vehicle for the ride back to the small Oklahoma town that David's mother called home.

Chapter 15

Upon returning to his mother's home, David joined her in the living room. This was the first time since David received her phone call that he could truly say he was relaxed. His mother told him to feel free to go and lie down. Although the thought of sleep tugged at David's mind, he decided to spend some time with his mother. She glanced over at the Christmas presents sitting in the corner of the room. She asked David his opinion as to what she should do with them. David told her to do nothing right now. He was sure his mother needed rest as much or more than he did. David's mother smiled at him. Her peculiar smile made David inquire to its cause. She told David that she was happy he was there with her. She commented on the first time his father fell ill and how appreciative she was for David, not just then but now as well. She told David that of all her children, he was the one she prayed would be there with her today. David consoled his mother and said he would always be there when she needed him. He then kissed his mother's head and took her up on the offer of rest. David walked down the short hall, entered the room, shut the door tightly behind him and laid down on the bed.

The room in which David was to stay was his mother's own. As he gazed around, he saw mementos of his parent's life together. On his mother's night stand David saw a picture she had framed and placed there. It was a photo of David on his first Little League team. David leaned over and picked up the picture in order to examine it more closely. The colors of the picture had faded but, for being nearly three decades old by now, David marveled at how well maintained his mother had kept it. David placed the picture back. As he pulled his hand away, Moses leapt up at David's arm. He had been hiding in wait under the bed. David took a moment to scratch his assailant's belly before leaning back on the bed and closing his eyes. The bed on which David laid was soft and warm. Soon David succumbed to his exhaustion and fell into a deep sleep.

David awoke a few hours later. He pulled himself to his

feet and made his way into the bathroom. Moses followed him. David placed some more food into his cat's dish. Moses purred and began to devour the food immediately. David turned the knobs of the sink. The water he splashed on his face was cool and refreshing. He dried his face and was walking out of the room when suddenly stopped. In his haste before David had not noticed his father's personal items resting on top of a tall dresser against the wall. His father's wallet, pocket knife and pocket watch were all there, as if awaiting their owner's return. David picked up the watch. His father had always been a pocket watch man. David remembered giving his father this very watch many years ago as a Christmas present. This reminded David that it was indeed Christmas. The first one without his father. There would be no more telling of the nativity story on Christmas Eve. No more jokes and laughter as presents were handed out on Christmas morning. His father was gone. David realized how much he now missed his father's presence. There had never been an open, loving relationship between them. The love they shared was understood to exist without expression. David had never minded this arrangement until now. He wished that he would have told his father that he loved him more often. At least he should have said it when his parents departed Florida instead of merely shaking his father's hand. David placed the watch back and left the room.

Chapter 16

David's mother was reading in her husband's large recliner. Upon seeing David walk in, she placed a mark in her book and set it down. She inquired if David had a good nap. He said he had. His mother told him to tell her about his trip. David recounted the drive he had only that morning finished. The long night; Moses's troubles with traveling; the empty cities. David did not, however, mention the prayers. It was not the time to bring up something like that, David thought. He was fairly sure his mother was aware he did not go to church. With their loss today, why should he cause his mother further anxiety? No, David would keep that to himself. He would maintain his charade. Now was the time for joyful tales not religious introspections. His mother said that she had still been wondering what to do with the Christmas presents. David responded that she should open them. They had been given by his father to her with love in his heart, hadn't they? Although he was gone, the love his father shared should never be extinguished. "I guess you're right." his mother replied. David crawled over to where he could reach the presents. He handed the first one up to his mother. She opened it slowly. It was a book that she had wanted. David's mother told him of how she had casually mentioned it to his father. Then, a few days later, a box came in the mail which his father immediately hid. It was impossible to keep secrets after fifty years, but the joy of the gift and its anticipation were all that really mattered. David handed another present up to his mother, who repeated the same pattern of slowly opening it then telling David its story.

As David listened, he suddenly felt very close to his father. He imagined sitting silently and watching his father perform the very action that David himself now did. David and his mother laughed over the stories. When all of his mother's presents were opened, David rose and again sat on the couch. His mother said that she would make David some dinner. David told her that it wasn't necessary, but she had already stood and crossed into the kitchen. Cooking was not a chore for David's mother, but a joy. Besides, David had not eaten his mother's cooking in many years. He followed his mother into the kitchen so that they could continue their conversation.

After a wonderful dinner of baked chicken and homemade bread, David and his mother again sat with each other in the living room. Tomorrow, the funeral preparations would begin. David said that he and his sister would go to the funeral home with her and handle it all. Christmas was almost over. David apologized to his mother that he had no gifts for her or his sister. David's mother laughed. The only gift she wanted, she told her son, was him there to share the day with her. David embraced his mother in the large recliner. He told his mother that he loved her. She told David that she was very proud of him. This was not something David had expected. He always thought his mother was disappointed in him for his falling away from the church and the religion his mother held so dear. The life he now led was not one that his mother would approve. Yet here his mother was, after such a great loss, telling her son that she was proud of him. A tear fell from

David's eye, but he wiped it away before his mother could see. David sat back on the couch. He noticed his mother appeared very tired. He asked her if she wanted to go to bed. She said that she was going to sleep in the recliner tonight. It was where David's father always slept. Due to health reasons, she told David, his father had never been able to sleep in the bed. David kissed his mother good night and wished her a merry Christmas. She smiled at her son and asked David to hand her the Bible on the small bookcase in the hall. David retrieved it. She told David she read from it every night. Even at a time like this, David's mother told him, she could always find comfort in its pages. The words never changed but life always did. David smiled and told his mother he loved her once more; then retired again to the room prepared for him.

David opened his small suitcase. He removed the toothbrush and toiletries he had packed in his haste. He proceeded to go through the nightly ritual of brushing his teeth and cleaning himself. As he did this, David thought about his mother out in the living room, reading her Bible before she herself retired for the night. He knew his mother must have read the entire Bible countless times. He could not imagine what new comfort she possible could find in its pages at this time. David finished and lied down on the bed. His mother had a small television sitting against the wall. He picked up the remote and turned on the television. David flipped through the channels until he found a station giving the local weather information. Tomorrow was to be a beautiful day, the anchor said. Highs in the low fifties and no chance of rain. Upon hearing this, David shut off the television. His thoughts drifted to the bourbon he would normally be sipping in this late hour. Alcohol had been a mainstay in his life from the time his faith had disappeared. Tonight however, David was not missing it as much as he anticipated he would. The day's events had left him too drained to dwell on imbibing. He flipped the light switch, plunging the room into darkness. As David made himself comfortable, he again felt the familiar form of Moses curling up next to him. Moses always preferred to sleep next to David's head back in Orlando, so it was little surprise that his furry companion would do the same here, so far from his home. In a matter of moments, the two travelers drifted off into a deep sleep.

Chapter 17

    That night David had a dream. Normally, the tumbler of bourbon and ice before bed kept him from remembering any dreams. Tonight, without the liquor's repressive effects, a vivid dream filled David's mind. He was a small boy. He was playing in the yard of his family's old house back in Florida. David tossed a baseball up in the air to himself then attempted to catch it in his small glove. He dropped as many as he caught. A voice came from behind him. David's father stood there. He asked David if he would like to play catch. David beamed with joy. His father worked hard and rarely played catch with him. David and his father threw the baseball back and forth. When David missed, his father would remind him to concentrate and keep his eye on the ball. As the baseball flew back and forth, David dropped it less and less. Finally David's father said it was time to stop. He congratulated his boy on a job well done. David ran over and hugged his father around the legs with his eyes closed.

David felt his father's large, strong hand rub him on the top of his head. When David opened his eyes again, he was no longer a small boy but an adult once more. He searched for his father but he was no longer there. David stood in the yard alone. The isolation here began to overwhelm David. Why had his father left him so alone? An unseen voice answered David's silent plea. The voice merely replied,"My son, why have you have left me?"

David awoke with a start. It was morning. To David, the dream had lasted the entire night. His body still felt tired from his journey. He sat up on the edge of the bed. Moses, who had been sleeping next to him, stretched and pushed his head against David's side. Rubbing his eyes, David attempted to shake the lingering memory of the dream. It had seemed so real. He had long ago forgotten the joy he had known as a child by playing catch with his father. In recent years, it had become a bit of a running joke between the two of them. Every week when David called his parents, his father would ask him when he was coming out so they could have a catch. The health of

David's father made this impossibility, of course. David was shaken that this, above all else, would be what he dreamed. David thought about the end of his dream. The voice was strange. David's father had a deep, commanding intonation but the voice in David's dream was gentle and almost remorseful. It was a voice that sounded strange, yet comforting at the same time. David pondered this as he sat on the edge of the bed. He remained lost in his thoughts until a gentle knock came to the door. His mother's voice asked him if he was awake. David replied that he was. His mother informed him that she was beginning to prepare breakfast and his sister and brother-in-law were on their way over to join them. David told his mother he would be right there. He stood and went into the bathroom to feed Moses and wash away the effects of the night and the dream it had given him.

Chapter 18

As David entered his mother's kitchen, the smell of frying bacon filled his nostrils. David embraced his mother, who asked her son how he had slept. David told his mother that he slept like a rock. He decided that this was not the time to discuss the dream. This was the time for breakfast. This was the meal that David had always cherished at Christmas time. David told his mother that he would be honored if he could make the scrambled eggs. Being a single man in his thirties, David had become a fair cook in his own right. As he whipped the eggs together in a bowl, David's sister and her husband arrived. The family, unified as best as they could in this time, was together again. David cooked the eggs on his mother's stove as his sister set the table. The mood in the air was light. They all talked about what their lives were now like. His sister was a school teacher. His brother-in-law worked in human resources at a local factory. David was careful in his speech. He kept his conversation limited to his work and friends that his mother remembered from when she lived near to him in Florida. When the food was finished cooking, the four family members sat around their mother's table. It was a place David had not been in many years. David reached for some toast but stopped himself. Everyone had their heads bowed in preparation for the meal's blessing. David had not blessed his food since he was a boy living with his parents. He worried his mother would ask him to speak. Did he even remember? His fear was dismissed when his brother-in-law began to pray. At the blessing's conclusion, the family members joined each other and began to partake. As David placed the first bite into his mouth, he marveled at the beauty of its taste.

As the meal neared its conclusion, David's brother-in-law filled him in as to what would have to be accomplished today. They had an appointment in about thirty minutes at the funeral home. Then they would have to go to the city's chamber of commerce and obtain the grave site. David said he would be happy to help any way he could. His mother informed them she was joining them at the funeral home but she could not go to the chamber of commerce. Some of the members of her church were stopping by later and she wanted to be sure she was at home when they arrived. David excused himself in order to get better dressed for the day's activities. He went back into his room and closed the door. He removed a pair of dress pants and a sweater out of his small suitcase. In the haste to leave his apartment, he hadn't folded these clothes. Wrinkles and creases lined his pants in every direction. David shrugged. What could be done at this point? At least, David thought, he wouldn't be around when the church members visited his mother. He feared being asked about his own faith. He was sure his mother was aware he no longer attended but David didn't feel like explaining himself to strangers. He would let his mother handle it. After all, these were her friends and her acquaintances. David had enough on his mind without acting like someone he no longer was for people he would most likely never meet again. He finished getting dressed and went back out to join his family.

Chapter 19

   The drive to the funeral home was short. This town was

so small that every place was only a short drive from any other.

David smiled to himself. This place reminded him of Mayberry

from the old Andy Griffith show. A simple country town that

had exactly what was required for its citizens to live but no

more. As David walked next to his mother into the funeral

home, they were immediately greeted by the home's director.

The director knew the family already and greeted David with a

warm smile and handshake. David quickly surmised that

everything up to this point had already been taken care of by

his sister and brother-in-law. All the better, David thought. It

was less he himself would have to do. The family sat around a

large table as the funeral director went to retrieve the necessary

paperwork. David held his mother's hand. She was full of

strength. David wondered how she was able to do this. Less

than twenty-four hours before, she had watched her husband of

almost fifty years pass away, yet here she was- clear-headed

and ready for anything. The director came back. He joined

David and his family around the table and began the long series of questions that must be asked. Most were routine. What casket would they like? Where was the service to be? What day? Then came the question that David had feared. David's father had been transported to the funeral home last night, but the director asked who would come to dress the body for the funeral service. Being the only son of his father there, David swallowed hard into the back of his throat. He didn't know how he could handle seeing his father now.

Before David could speak, however, his mother said that the reverend of her church had already made arrangements to come by later that day. David was taken back. His mother hadn't mentioned this to him. He wasn't even asked. His mother continued to explain to the director that certain sacred prayers and blessings had to be recited when the body was being prepared for eternal rest. David's brother-in-law mentioned he would be joining the reverend and two other men of the church and not to worry about a thing. The news hit

David like a brick. He realized he had not been asked because his mother did indeed know her son fell away from the church. She knew he never prayed. She knew his Bible was lost in the deep recesses in his closet. She knew her own son, her husband's flesh and blood, had himself made the decision long ago not to be worthy for this moment. David suddenly felt a deep regret. The remainder of the time he spent in the funeral home was in silence. David looked into his mother's eyes. Nothing but the deepest love was reflected back. Somehow, the thought of his mother loving him so completely, yet all the while knowing all about his lifestyle, made David feel even worse.

Chapter 20

His mother returned to her home while David continued

on with his sister and brother-in-law to the chamber of

commerce. No one spoke of the funeral home again. His sister

chronicled to David the story of her adopted hometown as they

drove. David noticed an abandoned theater and inquired his

sister about it. She said that it had been one of the best regional

theaters in the county back in the fifties but had fallen, as

buildings tend to do, into disrepair. David mentioned that he

would give anything to own such a building back home. To be

able to restore it to its former glory would be a labor of love.

David's sister said it was too far gone to ever be returned to a

state such as that. David responded that nothing is ever too far

gone if you want to restore it badly enough. His sister merely

shrugged her shoulders. David thought about what he had just

said. He remembered his dream. David remembered the voice

that spoke to him. He thought about not being asked to assist with his father at the funeral home. These contemplations built up in David's mind until his brother-in-law pulled into the parking lot of a small building. The sound of the engine shutting off snapped David back to where he was and what he was doing. The three family members exited the vehicle and walked towards the building.

David followed his sister and brother-in-law into the small building. David asked where they were. His sister told him that this was the chamber of commerce. David laughed. This was it? Back in Orlando, the chamber of commerce was an immense, multi-story hive of bureaucratic activity. This building appeared as abandoned as the theater which caught David's eye earlier. David's brother-in-law rang a bell on the counter. David's disbelief in his situation grew as a tiny old woman appeared from a back room. She was barely five feet tall and wore thick bifocals over her eyes. David's brother-in-law greeted the woman by name. She smiled and asked how David's mother was doing. His sister replied that she was well considering the circumstances. The tiny woman then greeted

David warmly. She said that she had heard much about him from his mother. Her husband, the woman continued, regularly had coffee with David's father. It was her husband, in fact, who had been the one to call the ambulance when David's father collapsed. She shook her tiny, gray-haired head and remarked what a shame it was to lose such a fine man. David hadn't realized how close this community really was.

The tiny woman set a large piece of cardboard onto the counter. On it was pasted a map of the local cemetery. Simple cross marks made with a ball-point pen indicted which plots were already purchased and which were still available. David's brother-in-law inquired about an area which was largely unmarked. The woman said this was a newer parcel in the cemetery and quite beautiful. She pointed to a particular section. She said that it was higher up on the hill and overlooked the valley below. David, having never seen the cemetery himself, trusted in his sister and her husband's opinion. They agreed that this spot would be perfect. David's brother-in-law informed the woman that they needed to pay for two plots today. That way, David's mother would be taken care of at the time of her passing. The tiny woman took her ballpoint pen and marked off the area, reserving it for David's father and mother. As she was writing out the check, David's sister remarked that it would be nice if they could afford two more plots for herself and her husband. The tiny woman behind the counter interjected that not only was it possible but also she would do it right now. Money, the woman continued, was no problem. David's sister and her husband could just drop by and pay what they could each month until the total amount had been achieved. David could scarcely believe his own ears. The trust this woman afforded them was truly amazing. As the three left the chamber of commerce, David remarked how in his home city, this process would have taken the entire day and, without a full credit check, payments would never had been an option. Perhaps some aspects of small town life remained something of which to be envious. This level of trust was definitely one of them.

Chapter 21

David was being dropped back off at his mother's house. His sister and brother-in-law had work to do, but they told David that they would return later for him and their mother. Their other sister was arriving at the airport later that evening. They would all drive together to pick her up and then have dinner out at a restaurant. David agreed and said he would relay this information to their mother. He stepped out and the vehicle drove away.

David noticed two cars parked along the street opposite of his mother's home. Undoubtedly, David thought, these belonged to members of his mother's church. This was the exact situation that David had wished to avoid. He had grossly underestimated the time that would be taken up at the chamber of commerce. Drawing up his breath, David knocked then entered his mother's home.

David had expected to be greeted by a few older ladies

comforting his mother. Instead there were two couples, both around David's own age. His mother introduced her son to these people. She told David that they were friends of hers and both very active in her church. Moses had made his way out of the bedroom and onto his mother's lap, where she stroked his fur to his vast enjoyment. David took a seat on the couch as the couples continued to tell him more about themselves. Both had multiple children. The two wives worked on many church-organized charity committees with David's mother. The men both worked on city councils. Not in the small town in which David's mother lived but for separate, larger cities nearby. David told them about his work in the theme park in Orlando. They marveled and remarked how wonderful it must be to have a job that brings so much joy to so many. David told them it was.

His mother then went into a detailed story about David's work in local theaters. David himself took this time to examine these people. How happy they seemed to be! David had never married, much less had children. He always felt sorry when he saw couples in the park his age, towing children by the hand. He imagined it must be terrible to be tied down, to know no freedom. Yet these two couples seemed not bound by life, but more joyous than David in his ever was. David said little more until the two couples stood to leave. Moses leapt from David's mother and raced back into the room. David shook the men's hands and told them how grateful he was that his mother had them and the church to support her. David was surprised not that he had said these words, but that he had actually meant them. He was happy his mother had her church. He never realized how much meaning it gave to her. David had grown to think of the church as merely an organization that gave false hope in exchange for fool's money. He now saw the peace and happiness his mother felt. The two couples left. As his mother closed the door and turned back, David embraced her. He told his mother that he loved her. David's mother told him she knew.

Chapter 22

The drive to the Oklahoma City airport was long. David had not seen this sister in quite some time, although he remained close to her through e-mail. She, David believed, was the most practical and level-headed of all his siblings. He was glad that she was the one who would take his place with their mother when he drove back home in the morning. She was strong. He believed his mother still needed that at this time.

David's sister was waiting for them as they pulled up to the airport. David jumped out to help with her suitcases. The two climbed back in the vehicle and they all drove away. David's sister told them all about her trip. Apparently she had been afraid of a delay due to the holiday but her flight left and arrived without a hitch. Snow at her departing airport, which had also been predicted to cause delays, had not fallen. David's mother said that God was definitely guiding her way, to which everyone in the vehicle agreed. David asked her about her work. She said she had the weekends off already, so missing these days was not an issue. David's brother-in-law asked them all where they wanted to eat. The choice, the siblings decided, was to be their mother's. She chose a popular restaurant nearer to her home. They agreed and drove out of the city.

After finishing their much-needed meal, the family returned to their mother's home. The hours of the day had vanished. David's mother retired to a spare room where she was sleeping that night. David knew he should also try to get as much sleep as possible. He was now all too aware of the miles he would have to face tomorrow. Before he departed for bed, however, David's sister pulled him aside. She asked David how their mother was really handling the situation. David filled her in on the details of the previous two days. He even mentioned how much the church had been helping. His sister, who had always remained active in the church, remarked that she was never in doubt of this. David again thanked his sister. Then David's sister embraced him. This was not something for which David had been prepared. His sister was very stoic by nature and seldom even shook her brother's hand. The warmth of this unexpected embrace comforted David. She told him to be safe on his journey and remember that God was with him always. David thanked his sister then went into the room that was prepared for him. Shutting the door tightly behind him, David dropped to his knees at the side of the bed. Unable to control his emotions any longer, he wept into his hands. David found himself praying again. He prayed for his family. He prayed for his safety. Then David sought the depths of his heart and, through the tears wetting his face, David asked for forgiveness. He remembered every drink he had, every woman he had slept with, every day he slept while others went to church and of every indiscretion he committed. David then drew himself up to where Moses was waiting and passed out on the bed of his mother.

That night David had another dream. He was again a small boy with his father. They were walking down the sandy beach bordering a lake in which David used to swim. This time, however, they were not alone. David's small right hand was held securely by his father, who smiled down at his young son. David's other hand was held in a similar fashion by a man David did not recognize but felt a deep love for anyway. This other man smiled down at David. David smiled back up at the man. The man spoke to David. It was the same voice from his dream the night before. The man merely said,"Welcome back."

Chapter 23

David arose to leave at 5:30 the next morning. His mother was waiting for him. She hugged her son with tears in her eyes, thanking him from the bottom of her heart for his being there. David too cried as he told his mother again and again that he loved her. When he could wait no longer, David picked up Moses's belongings and his suitcase and walked out to his truck. The morning air was frigid and ice had formed on the windshield. David started his truck and began the process of scraping the ice away. When he was finished, David walked back into his mother's home. His mother held out her hand to her son. In her fist she held her husband's pocket watch. She told David that it was now his and to forever remember that his father loved him. David said he always would. David placed the cherished watch in his pocket and picked up Moses, who was terrified again at the thought of the long journey. David took Moses and set him back into the truck, which was now quite warm. Moses hid himself back down under the seat. David blew his mother a kiss before climbing in himself. As he pulled away into the dark, cold morning, David watched his mother wave goodbye to him in his rearview mirror.

David arrived back at his apartment nineteen hours and forty-seven minutes later. He had used all this time to reflect upon his odyssey. He thought of his father and of what his father had truly meant to him. He thought of the dreams he had experienced. Mostly though, David used these near twenty hours alone to think about how his prayer the night before affected him. David felt different now. He felt as if a weight had been lifted from his back. The distance he had placed between himself and his family throughout the years seemed to have vanished over mere days. He felt connected again with something he had lost but never knew he missed. David thought about all these things over and over again.

He opened the door to his small apartment. Moses sprang from his arms and ran around his home, so happy to have returned. David threw himself onto his couch. He had imagined drinking a large glass of bourbon and passing out for as long as possible. Instead, he took his father's watch out and placed it on the table in front of him. As he stared at the pocket watch, David drew himself back up on his exhausted legs. He went into his bedroom and opened the closet door. David began going through the boxes in the back of his closet. Some of these boxes hadn't been opened since David moved in several years ago. Finally, after several minutes and several boxes, David found what sought. He held a thick, brown book in his hands. David went back out to his couch and sat down. He gazed at the cover of the book. In gold type on the cover were two simple words: Holy Bible. David opened the dusty cover and began to read.